More Thoughts

A Freewriting Journal

Janet Morey
Gail Schafers

PRO LINGUA  ASSOCIATES

Contents

Journal of your thoughts 1
Your teacher's responses 88
Index of prompts 110

Pro Lingua Associates, Publishers

P.O. Box 1348
Brattleboro, Vermont 05302-1348 USA
Office: 802 257 7779
Orders: 800 366 4775
E-mail: orders@ProLinguaAssociates.com
SAN: 216-0579

Webstore: www.ProLinguaAssociates.com

Copyright © 2015 by Janet Morey and Gail Schafers

ISBN 13: 978-0-86647-368-2; 10: 0-86647-368-8

The book was set and designed by A.A. Burrows, in close collaboration with the authors, using Adobe's Times New Roman, a variant of one of the most popular type faces of the modern era. Originally it was created for *The Times* of London in 1931 by Victor Lardent and Stanley Morison. Its history is complicated and litigious. Linotype, working with *The Times*, registered it as Times Roman; Monotype, which originally issued the type, called it Times New Roman. Microsoft, Apple, and Adobe all have digital variants. All the variations are strong, easy-to-read serif fonts. The design of the cover uses a photograph of Red Velvet © Samantha Grandy from Dreamstime.com. Other photos from that agency are: on p 17 snacks © Aleksander Pulios, p 18 grasshopper @ Greir11p 28 Chinese New Years at home © Szefel, p 32 woman with her dog, © Andres Rodriquez, p 39 Maya Moore © Daniel Raustadt and David Ortiz © Ronald Callaghan, p 64 Serekaniye, Syria, bombed © Fatih Polat, U.S. soldier © Oleg Zabielin, and Aleppo © Richard Harvey, p 74 ghost stair @ Daver0316, 75 Cat © Imrich Farkas, p 79 Iguana © Alekoho, p 80 Anime girl in Hong Kong © Kuan Leong Yong, and on p 81 Dragon warror boy crouching © Algol.

This book was printed and bound by King Printing Co., Inc. in Lowell, Massachusetts. Printed in the United States.   First edition 2015   500 copies in print

Other Books by Janet Morey and Gail Schafers
My Thoughts: A Freewriting Journal
Talk and Write! A Photocopyable Collection of Writing Activies

Yesterday you found a note in a bottle
that had washed onto the shore.
What did the message say? What will you do?

You were hiking in the mountains.
You turned a corner and suddenly saw . . .

What happened?

Suddenly you discover you have a day off.
Would you go fishing, sailing, hiking, or biking? Or ?
Describe your day.

You did it! You climbed a very tall mountain.
How do you *feel*, and what do you *see* and *hear*?

You receive a text message from your friend,
and it makes you feel happy.
What is the story behind the message?

You moved into an old house; you see a door
you hadn't noticed before. You open the door . . .
What do you see?

You can change your name officially.
What name will you choose?
OR will you stick with the name you have?

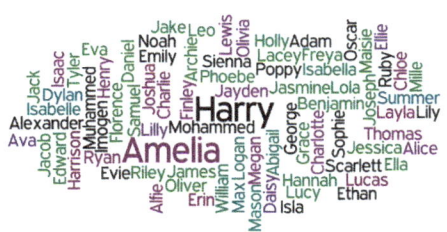

Jump in the car. Put down the top. Put on your sunglasses. Where will you go? Who will go with you?

Jump in the old truck. Where will you go?
Who will go with you?

10

List five things you want to
do before you die.
Choose one and explain why.

Do clowns make you laugh? Why or why not?

Describe a dark and stormy night and how you feel
when the wind roars and the thunder booms.

Would you enjoy living in a tiny house like this?

Why or why not?

Imagine that you are walking along a quiet country lane. Using as many of the five senses as you can, write about your feelings.

Imagine that you are walking along a noisy city street. Using as many of the five senses as you can, write about your feelings.

Write about a memory connected with a taste
– either a good taste or a bad one.

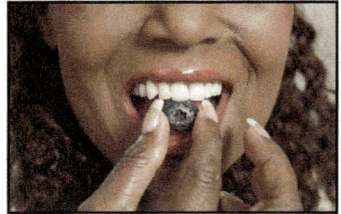

The head of your school has asked you
to plan a snack bar that serves only healthy food.
Describe your menu.

Some people in the world eat grasshoppers.
Would you? What insects would you eat? How
would you cook them, or would you eat them raw?

Who do you love and why?

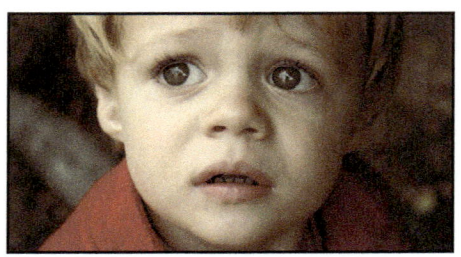

What scared you at night when you were little?

You meet a person who can tell your future
by reading the palm of your hand.
What does she tell you about your future?

A fishing shack? a park? a beach? a coffee shop?
a bakery? a room?
Close you eyes and visualize your favorite place.
Write about the sounds, smells, tastes, and
feelings you remember.

Define solitude. How do you like
to spend your "solitude"?

What does your favorite color look like,
sound like, taste like, smell like, and feel like?

What is the most special gift
you have ever received? Was it expensive,
inexpensive, or free, such as a plate of cookies?
Describe it and write what it meant to you.

Congratulations! You have won a trip for two
on a magical horse. You can go anywhere in the world.
Where will you go, and who will you take with you?

Your grandfather gave you an old teddy bear. Last night as you got ready for bed, the bear began to talk to you. What did it say?

Describe the best thing about your yesterday.

Which musical instrument have you always
loved and wished you could play? Why?

Are you "wise as an owl,"
or "quiet as a mouse," or "busy as a bee?"
Select any adjective that describes you
and explain your choice.

What do you think and do when you see
a rainbow?

What is your best memory of a past holiday?

Write about your neighborhood
OR about a neighborhood special to you –
either past or present.

Cats purr when they are contented;
dogs wag their tails. How do YOU show your
happiness, and what do you do?

If you had a robot,
what would you want it to do for you?

An old saying goes, "A dog is a man's best friend."
Can a dog be a best friend to a person?

What happened here?

What is this young woman thinking?

What made this child happy yesterday?

A big dog chased your cat, and she climbed up to the highest branches of a tall, tall tree. She can't get down. What will you do?

Who lives in this small cottage? Write a detailed description of the resident(s).

You are sitting in a coffee shop,
and you hear someone say, "It was the worst day
of my life." Imagine what happened to this person.

Who is your favorite athlete? What do you respect about this person, both professionally and personally?

Maya Moore

Big Papi David Ortiz

44

What did the person who wore these shoes do today?

What did the person who wore these work boots
do today?

Imagine you are a bus driver. Describe some of the people who get on your bus every day.

This alien visited your classroom and described life on its planet.
What did it tell you?

You are a portrait in a busy art museum. Describe some of the people who passed by and studied you during one hour yesterday.

An oak tree stands tall and strong. A willow is delicate and bendable. A palm faces storms courageously. Who reminds you of a tree and why?

Your aunt asks you to meet her at a coffee shop.
She wants to tell you a family secret.
What does she tell you?

Create a story about this picture.

Create a story about this picture.

Create a story about this picture.

Create a story about this picture.

Describe a beautiful lake, ocean, river, brook, or creek, and your experience there.

Alligator snapping turtles are endangered in some states. Many people think they are ugly, so would it really matter if they disappeared forever?

What's your opinion?

What is your opinion of insects and spiders?

Are they funny . . beautiful, . . interesting . .
frightening . . disgusting ?
Write about one of these creatures.

Describe the beauty (?) of an alligator.

What do you imagine this
baby bird is feeling?
Do you feel that way sometimes?
Explain when and why.

We talk about the beauty of nature,
but nature can be cruel. A tornado is an example.
How will you protect yourself
if you see a tornado coming?

We read about fracking, strip-mining, and clear-cutting, all of which threaten our environment. Choose one of these practices and tell what we can do to reduce these threats to nature.

Write about the wonder of a starry night without using the words "sky" or "star."

Tigers are critically endangered. People kill them for their skins and for medicinal purposes. Write a letter to the hunters, and persuade them to stop hunting.

What advice would you give to a friend who is being bullied?

Should school administrators set dress codes?
Should caps, short-short skirts, and baggy pants
be banned? Why or why not?

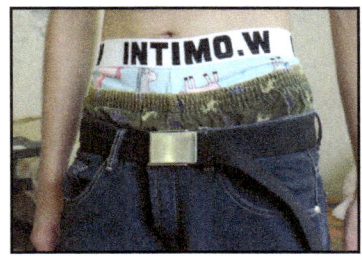 

When you see a homeless person begging,
how do you feel, and what do you do?

Do you believe that aliens have visited earth?
Why or why not?

War . . . What is it good for? . . .
Absolutely nothing*. . .

Is there anything good that comes out of a war?

*From a song by Edwin Starr.

"Music was my refuge. I could crawl into the space between the notes and curl my back to loneliness."

Poet and author Maya Angelou

What kind of music provides "refuge" for you? Please explain.

70

Poet Langston Hughes wrote:

Let the rain kiss you . . .
*Let the rain sing you a lullaby . . .**

Tell what you love to do – inside or outside
– on a rainy day.

*From *April Rain Song*.

Poet Robert Frost wrote:

> *I have been one acquainted with the night.*
> *I have walked out in rain – and back in rain.*
> *I have outwalked the furthest city light . . .* *

Describe a time when you were alone at night – either at home or outside.

*From *Acquainted with the Night*

My river grows dark and still at night in the fall;
The waves are calm, ready for sleep.
I drop in my line,
But the fish, too, are sleeping.

My empty boat and I turn to the shore
Filled with our catch
*of moonlight.**

Write about an experience you had in a boat.

*By Li Jung, 16th century Korea.
Re-created by A. A. Burrows

In her poem *There is no frigate like a book,* Emily Dickinson wrote:

There is no frigate like a book
To take us lands away . . .

What is the best book you have ever read, and where did it take you in imagination?

*A frigate is a fast warship.

"While I nodded, nearly napping, suddenly there came a tapping,
As of someone gently rapping, rapping at my chamber door.
"'Tis some visitor,' I muttered, 'tapping at my chamber door...'"

You are home alone. You hear someone "rapping" at your door.
You go to the door and open it.
Who is there? What happens next?

From Edgar Allan Poe's *The Raven*

As I was going up the stair,
I met a man who wasn't there.
He wasn't there again today.
I wish that he would go away!

Explain who the mysterious man on the "stair" was.

A nursery rhyme by Hughes Mearns, 1899.

In his poem *Tree house*, Shel Silverstein wrote:

> *A street house, a neat house*
> *Be sure to wipe your feet house*
> *Is not my kind of house at all –*
> *Let's go live in a tree house . . .*

Would you live in a tree house? Why or why not?

Today is a smooth white seashell.
Hold it close, and listen to the beauty
of the hours. – Anonymous

Write about a sound that brought "beauty" to your "hours."

From Poet A.A. Burrows: *Fall is winding down,*
Stripping the trees,
Sweeping the color into piles
Beneath the bushes . . .
It's almost time to sleep.

Seasons change in different ways around the world. Choose one of these transitional times, and explain how it affects your mood.

In his poem *Miracles,* Walt Whitman lists the many "miracles" that surround us every day. Here are a few:

As to me, I know of nothing else but miracles,
Whether I walk the streets of Manhattan...
Or watch honey-bees busy around the hive...
Or stand a long while looking at the movements of machinery...
The fishes that swim—the rocks—the motion of the
        waves—the ships, with men in them . . . ,

Describe an everyday "miracle" that you especially love.

From poet Henry Van Dyke:

...Time is
Too Slow for those who Wait,
Too Swift for those who Fear,
Too Long for those who Grieve,
Too Short for those who Rejoice,
* But for those who Love,*
*   Time is not.*

What "time" above best describes your feelings right now?

From *For Katrina's Sun-Dial*

More Thoughts

More Thoughts

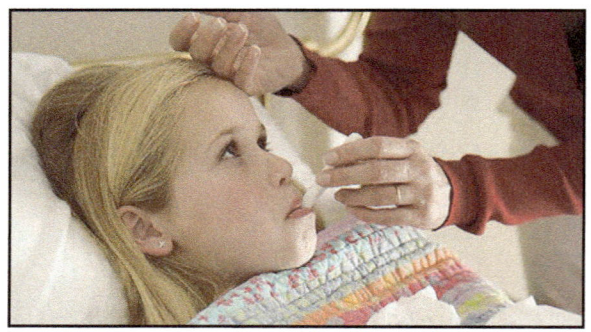

More Thoughts

More Thoughts

More Thoughts

More Thoughts

A Last Thought

Yesterday you found a note in a bottle? • 1

You were hiking in the mountains. • 2

Suddenly you discover you have a day off. • 3

You climbed a very tall mountain. How do you *feel*? • 4

You receive a text message from your friend. • 5

You moved into an old house: you see a door... • 6

You can change your name officially. • 7

Jump in the car. Where will you go? • 8

Jump in the old truck. Where will you go? • 9

List five things you want to do before you die. • 10

Do clowns make you laugh? • 11

Describe a dark and stormy night and how you feel. • 12

Would you enjoy living in a tiny house like this? • 13

Imagine that you are walking along a quiet country lane. • 14

Imagine that you are walking along a noisy city street.. • 15

Write about a memory from your childhood connected with a taste. • 16

Snack bar with healthy food. • 17

Some people eat grasshoppers • 18

Who do you love and why?. • 19

What scared you at night when you were a child? • 20

You meet a person who can tell your future. • 21

A fishing shack? a park? ... your favorite place. • 22

Write about solitude. • 23

What does your favorite color look like ... and feel like? • 24

What is the most special gift you have ever received? • 25

You have won a trip for two on a magical horse. • 26

Your grandfather gave you an old teddy bear. • 27

Describe the best thing about your yesterday. • 28

Which musical instrument have you always loved? Why? • 29

Are you "wise as an owl"? • 30

What do you think and do when you see a rainbow? • 31

What is your best memory of a past holiday? • 32

Write about your neighborhood. • 33

Cats purr . . . How do YOU show your happiness? • 34

If you had a robot, what would you want it to do for you? • 35

An old saying goes, "A dog is a man's best friend." • 36

What happened here? • 37

What is this young woman thinking? • 38

What made this child happy yesterday? • 39

A big dog chased your cat. She can't get down. • 40

Who lives in this small cottage?. • 41

You are sitting in a coffee shop. • 42

Who is your favorite athlete? • 43

What did the person who wore these shoes do today? • 44

What did the person who wore these work boots do today? • 45

Imagine you are a bus driver. • 46

This alien visited your classroom. What did it tell you? • 47

You are a portrait in a busy art museum. • 48

Who reminds you of a tree and why? • 49

Your aunt asks you to meet her at a coffee shop. • 50

Create a story about this picture: Boy and dog. • 51

Create a story about this picture: Holding hands on beach. • 52

Create a story about this picture: Reading. • 53

Create a story about this picture: Looking out at the snow. • 54

Describe a beautiful lake, ocean, river, brook or creek and your experience. • 55

Alligator snapping turtles are endangered in some states. • 56

What is your opinion of insects and spiders? • 57

Describe the beauty (?) of an alligator. • 58

What is this baby bird feeling? • 59

Nature can be cruel. A tornado is an example. • 60

We read about fracking ... what we can do to reduce these threats. • 61

Write about the wonder of a starry night. • 62

Tigers are critically endangered. • 63

Advice to your friend who is being bullied • 64

Should school administrators set dress codes? • 65

When you see a homeless person begging... • 66

Do you believe that aliens have visited earth? • 67

Is there anything good that comes out of a war? • 68

Maya Angelou: *Music was my refuge.* • 75

Langston Hughes: *Let the rain kiss you.* • 69

Robert Frost: *I have been one acquainted with the night.* • 70

Li Jung/A.A. Burrows: *My river grows dark and still at night in the fall.* • 71

Emily Dickinson: *There is no frigate like a book.* • 72

Edgar Allan Poe's *The Raven.* • 73

Nursery rhyme: As I was going up the stair... • 74

Shel Silverstein: *Tree House.* • 76

Anonymous: *Today is a smooth white seashell.* • 77

A.A. Burrows: *Fall is winding down.* • 78

Walt Whitman: *Miracles..* • 79

Henry Van Dyke: *Time is.* • 80

More of my thoughts: Unicorn • 81

More of my thoughts: Fever • 82

More of my thoughts: Swing • 83

More of my thoughts: Dinosaur • 84

More of my thoughts: Lizard • 85

More of my thoughts: Manga girl • 86

A last thought: Manga boy • 87

Index of Prompts

A

aliens 47,67
alligator 58
alligator
   snapping
   turtle 56
alone 70
art museum 48
athlete 43

B

bear 2
biking 3
bird 59
boat 72
books 73
bullying 64
bus driver 46

C

cars 8, 37
cats 34, 40
childhood 20
clear cutting 61
clowns 11
coffee shop 42, 50
color 24
cookies 25
cooking 18
cottage 41
create a
   story 51-54
creek 55

D

day off 3
death 10
dogs 35, 40
door 6, 74
dress code 65

E

eating 18
endangered
   species 56, 63
the environment 61

F

fall 72, 78
favorites
   athlete 43
   color 24
   place 22
feelings 4, 14, 15
fishing 3, 72
fortune teller 21
fracking 61
friends 36, 64
the future 21

G

gifts 25
grasshopper 18

H

happiness 34
healthy food 17
hiking 2, 3
holiday 32
homeless 66
house 6,13, 76

I

insects 18, 57

L

lake 55
laughter 11
love 19

M

magical horse 26
memory 16
message 1, 5
miracles 79
mountains 2, 4
more thoughts
   81-87
music 69
musical
   instruments 29

N

names 7
neighborhood 33
night 12, 20, 62,
   71-72
note in a bottle 1

O

old house 6
ocean 55

P

poems 70-76,
   78-80

R

rain 70
rainbow 31
river 55, 72
robot 35

S

sailing 3
scared 20
secret 50
senses 4, 14,
   15, 24
shoes 44
snacks 17
solitude 23
sounds 77
spider 57
starry night 62
storm 12
strip mining 61

T

taste 16
teddy bear 27
text message 5
thinking 38
tiger 63
time 80
tornado 60
trees 49, 76
tree house 76
truck 9

V

visitor 74

W

war 68
work boots 45
worst day 42

Y

yesterday 28
you 30, 34